FOLLOWING THE SAVIOR ONE STEP AT A TIME

Christy Wilburn Nobella Webb

April 2023

Preface

When the Savior walked the earth, He encountered many who were anxious to hear the things He had to say. He recognized that the best way to teach gospel principles would be by sharing parables and experiences that they could easily relate to.

I have found that I am a person who also learns best when I read the parables Jesus taught, or I hear a talk where the speaker shares an experience that they have gone through that has helped them learn a gospel principle.

Some people have an easier time following the Savior one step at a time than others. Before I invite you to read this book where I share my own experiences, I would like you to know that I stumble as I try to follow the Savior. I find myself constantly biting my tongue before I say something and I often trip over my own temper. I have been surprised as I continue to get older that I am still working each day to not stumble, but to perfect my steps as I walk along life's pathways when I try to follow our Savior's example.

Each day we are all given a new opportunity to make a variety of choices. We can either choose to follow the Savior's example in our decision making, or we can choose a path that might lead us in a direction that may result in an outcome that may not be what we originally had in mind.

From time to time, we have all made choices that have been successful or resulted in choices that we regretted. In Part 1, I will be sharing some of my experiences where I have learned the value of following the Savior's example, as well as, presenting the benefits of striving each day to walk in His footsteps.

In Part 2, I will be sharing experiences where I put the Lord first and how my choices affected my life.

In Part 3, I will be sharing experiences where I learned that through giving service to others, I can receive ultimate joy and happiness.

It's comforting to know that we are not alone in our daily journeys. Heavenly Father has given us His Son who has shown us the way to a pathway of joy and contentment if we will choose to follow Him.

In each chapter I have shared a true story from my life, and in some cases, I have changed the names of the individuals. The scriptures used are from the authorized King James Version of the Bible for the Church of Jesus Christ of Latter-Day Saints and The Book of Mormon.

CDW Publishing

This year I am studying and reading The New Testament. As we enter the season where we commemorate our Savior's Atonement and Resurrection, I feel impressed to write this book and share how His influence has helped and guided my life. I am forever in His debt for His perfect example and for His willingness to give His precious life to atone for my sins. There are no words to express how truly thankful I am for His love and sacrifice. I will strive each day to be like Him and will gladly follow in His precious footsteps. I love you, dear Savior.

Christy Webb has been an avid reader all her life. She especially enjoys a fun romance with unexpected plot twists. Ever since she was a little girl, teachers and friends have begged her to share her funny life experiences by turning them into delightful and memorable fictional stories. She lives in Utah with her loving husband, who is the perfect role model for all of her heroes.

PART 1

The Value of Following the Savior's example and

The Benefits of Striving each day to walk in His footsteps

Chapter 1

My husband and I were attending our new church as newlyweds for the first time. I remember how reluctant I was to say goodbye to him after the main service was over and go to the women's meeting all by myself, not knowing a single person. Should I sit in the front of the room, or hide in the back, or maybe I could get lost in the shuffle if I chose a seat in the middle? Everyone was chatting and having a wonderful conversation, but no one even noticed I had made an entrance.

As I sat alone, twiddling my thumbs and trying to blend in, I thought about a conversation I had with my mother several years earlier. She always complimented me on my ability to talk to anyone, while she on the other-hand, was terribly shy and could never think of anything to say to someone.

I watched as a lady finally came and sat down by me and I waited, and waited some more wondering when she would ask me if I was new and welcome me to the women's meeting. I have to admit that when she never uttered a word, I was not liking this new church and couldn't wait to have a talk with my husband about moving and attending somewhere else that was more friendly.

My thoughts and future plans were interrupted when the meeting began and the lady conducting asked if there were any visitors or new members. To my great surprise, the lady next to me raised her hand and announced that she and her family had just moved into the area the same day as I had! I smiled to myself, while raising my hand, to advise everyone that I was also new and had just moved in too! I winked at the lady next to me and she smiled as well.

I learned a valuable lesson that day. If I was following in the Savior's footsteps, I would have introduced myself and not waited for someone to talk to me first. You never know when you may be sitting next to someone who is as new as you are!

Luke 10:27

And he answering said, Thou shalt love the Lord thy God with all thy heart, and with all thy soul, and with all thy strength, and with all thy mind; and thy neighbour as thyself.

Chapter 2

My sister, Lawanna, was two years older than me, and was full of life with a vibrant personality that matched her beautiful auburn hair. She had the most gorgeous green eyes that sparkled whenever she smiled, and I was definitely envious of the big dimple in her left cheek that magically appeared every time she smiled.

She loved our parents and always went out of her way to complete her chores in a timely manner, and if that wasn't enough, she spent the rest of her day trying to please them.

It wasn't surprising to discover that Lawanna had a talent for making friends. Everyone loved her and wanted to be included in her circle. She regularly received invitations to her friend's birthday parties and slumber parties. On one special occasion, when I was thirteen and she was fifteen, I was invited to attend a slumber party with her. I still remember how thrilled I was to be included and couldn't wait to attend!

I was having the time of my life at the party and the best was yet to come when we each began lining our sleeping bags and pillows into a large circle. I was informed that we were going to have a 'gossip' night and I had to pinch myself to make sure I wasn't dreaming. I couldn't believe I was actually going to be included in on all of the latest juiciest gossip!

The hostess of the party advised that she would be the first person to share a juicy tidbit about someone and then each of us would take a turn telling something juicy about anyone we knew. I was thoroughly enjoying the gossip as each person in the circle continued to share until it was my sister, Lawanna's turn to share something. I'll never forget what she said, and I have to admit I was mad at her for ruining the fun by saying, "Hey everyone, I have a great idea! Why don't we say what we like most about people and then keep it going around the circle."

Lawanna was so well-liked that everyone decided to follow her lead and the gossip stopped, being replaced by good things about the friends we knew. I learned a very important lesson that night from her example of following the Savior. She chose not to gossip; but instead, she shared the good qualities about the people she knew. I discovered why Lawanna had so many friends. She never spoke badly about anyone behind their back. If she did say something, it was always positive and uplifting.

Psalms 34:13

Keep thy tongue from evil, and thy lips from speaking guile.

Proverbs 11:13

A talebearer (gossip) revealeth secrets; but he that is of a faithful spirit concealeth the matter.

James 4:11

Speak not evil one of another, brethren. He that speaketh evil of his brother, and judgeth his brother, speaketh evil of the law, and judgeth the law: but if thou judge the law, thou art not a doer of the law, but a judge.

••

One more story about Lawanna...

Lawanna came down with the disease of MS (Multiple Sclerosis) at a young age in her married life and eventually had to go into an assisted living facility due to her complications from the disease.

Every Thanksgiving holiday, we would gather as sisters (there were five living sisters, including Lawanna), and we would go and visit her. It is difficult to watch one of your siblings struggle with a debilitating disease and we often felt guilty for being healthy. On one of our visits, she could sense our feelings of guilt over our good health and made the following comment; "I'm so glad that if one of us had to get this disease, it was me. I love each one of you so much and wouldn't want any of you to have to go through this. If I had to, I would volunteer to go through this so none of you would have to."

My sisters and I left that day loving her even more and realizing what a special sister we had been blessed with. Over the years her words have come back to me reminding me of our Savior who stated the same thing to our Father in Heaven in the pre-existence when He volunteered to come to earth to suffer and atone for our sins.

My sister, Lawanna, was a wonderful example of someone who knew how to follow our Savior's footsteps.

John 15:13

Greater love hath no man than this, that a man lay down his life for his friends.

Chapter 3

When I was in elementary school around the age of nine, I went outside to the playground after I had finished eating my lunch. While looking around for some friends to play with, a group of girls invited me to chase a boy named Billy who had a disability. Not seeing any of my friends, I joined in and began chasing him and calling him mean names.

I remember thinking to myself that what we were doing wasn't very nice, but I was bored and hadn't found my other friends, so I continued teasing him. We relentlessly chased poor Billy, calling him mean names, and soon he began to cry and ran inside the school building.

I felt terrible when I realized I was part of the group that was responsible for making him cry. While we were outside deciding what we would do next, Billy came outside followed by the school principal. When I saw the principal, I felt sick to my stomach and wished I hadn't made the choice to tease and torment Billy.

We all had to go to the principal's office where he explained Billy's disability and that it was impossible for him to control his bodily actions. I remember feeling even worse and worried about what the consequences of my actions would be.

The principal called my mother and informed her of my participation in the teasing of Billy. When I arrived home from school, she let me know that we would be having a talk about it after dinner. In our talk, she reminded me that I had been given a very special name of Chris and if I added a 't' to my name, it would spell the name of our Savior. Because of this fact, I had an even greater responsibility to make sure that I followed the Savior's example.

I definitely learned my lesson that day and have since made a conscious effort not to make fun of anyone again. There have been times in my own life where I was teased about things I couldn't control. It has been a good reminder of the day I teased, Billy, and how painful it is to be on the receiving end of someone else's teasing.

James 4:11

Speak not evil one of another brethren. He that speaketh evil of his brother, and judgeth his brother, speaketh evil of the law, and judgeth the law: but if thou judge the law, thou are not a doer of the law, but a judge.

Golden Rule

Do unto others as you would have them do unto you.

Matthew 7:12

Therefore all things whatsoever ye would that men should do to you, do ye even so to them; for this is the law and the prophets.

• •

Later that same year, I had an opportunity to choose to follow the Savior's footsteps and would like to share that experience.

In the church I grew up in, we used to have Friday afternoon/evening movies at our church building. One Friday, after I had taken a seat with my family and was waiting for the movie to start, I noticed Louise, a girl from my school who was sitting by herself. For some reason, no one liked Louise and if you associated with her and others saw you, you could be labeled unpopular too. I thought about the day I had chosen to tease Billy and wondered if I went and sat by Louise what would happen. I also knew that this would be a good opportunity to show Heavenly Father that I was sorry for my previous actions toward Billy. By being kind to Louise, I could now show Him how I was trying to follow in the Savior's footsteps.

I asked my mother if I could go and invite Louise to sit with us and she readily agreed. I can still remember the look of surprise on Louise's face when I invited her to sit with our family. She responded with, "Are you sure?" I nodded my head with a positive smile and she smiled back.

To this day, I can't remember what the movie was that night, but I still remember the wonderful feeling of love and joy that came over me because I had chosen to follow the Savior's footsteps and I'll never forget Louise's delighted smile.

John 15:12

This is my commandment, that ye love one another as I have loved you.

Chapter 4

I accepted a position to be the pianist for a young group of children in my church many years ago with the understanding that whomever was called to be the chorister would give me the assigned songs ahead of time so I would have several days to practice before having to perform them. I have always admired and been in awe of those pianists that can be handed a sheet of music and can play it perfectly without any practice. Unfortunately, I am not one of those pianists.

I found myself in a situation where the former chorister moved out of the area and a new chorister was called in her place. I looked forward to working with the new chorister so I could explain that I needed ample time to practice the songs in order to play them well before our Sunday school meeting.

To make a long story short, the new chorister had a very busy schedule and didn't have time to plan the songs we would be doing until the last minute. Many times, I received the list of songs five minutes before I was required to play them. As you can imagine, I stumbled through the music embarrassing myself.

One day when the chorister was trying to teach a new song and I continued to make one mistake after another, she made the following comment, "If we had a pianist that could play the piano, I might be able to teach you children the song." That was the straw that broke the camel's back for me. When Sunday school was over that day, I handed my music books in and quit. I also decided I needed a break from church.

For the next several weeks, I was on strike and didn't attend church. The first few weeks I felt justified in my decision. After that, I was just angry. A few more weeks went by and my Pastor set up an appointment to meet with me. Of course, I told him my tale of woe and when I finished, he asked, "What do you think the Savior would do?"

I was pretty upset with that question and hurriedly replied, "He would probably play the piano perfectly and wouldn't be in this mess!"

My Pastor smiled and then encouraged me to pray for the individual that had upset me. I couldn't believe he would ask me to pray for her when she was the one at fault. Shouldn't she be praying for me?

Thank goodness I had a very calm and loving Pastor. By the time our visit was over, I promised that I would faithfully pray every day for the individual whom I felt had wronged me. The Pastor promised that if I did that, I would feel the Savior's love for me and for the individual who had hurt my feelings.

I swallowed my pride and began to pray every night for the individual who had hurt my feelings, as well as myself, and I decided to go back to church. To my great surprise, my anger began to dissipate.

A few weeks later, the individual and I met in the hall on our way to various meetings, and I was surprised and relieved that I didn't feel the anger for her anymore. We hugged each other and apologized and all was forgiven.

I learned once again that when we put aside our ways and follow our Savior's example and footsteps, our paths become easier and more enjoyable.

Matthew 18:21-22

Then came Peter to him, and said, Lord, how oft shall my brother sin against me, and I forgive him? Till seven times?

Jesus saith unto him, I say not unto thee, Until seven times; but, Until seventy times seven.

Luke 11:4

And forgive us our sins; for we also forgive every one that is indebted to us. And lead us not into temptation; but deliver us from evil.

Chapter 5

Bearing my own children was not a blessing I was meant to have in this life. My husband and I were not blessed with our son, Jimmy, until the seventh year of our marriage. He came through the long process of adoption. We had just moved into a new area and were excited when we received an invitation from our new church members to go out to dinner with them and several other couples.

We had just finished a delightful dinner when the waitress arrived to see if any of us wanted to order dessert. All of the couples were ordering extravagant sundaes with all the works including ice cream, chocolate syrup, bananas, nuts, and brownies. I groaned inwardly because I had worked diligently the previous six months to lose over thirty pounds and was now faced with a difficult choice. I felt like I would gain weight from the sheer delight of looking at the delicious dessert.

One by one the waitress was taking dessert orders. When it was my turn to order, I declined and as the waitress walked away, one of the men stated; "I think it's a shame when a woman won't give up her figure to have a baby." My first reaction was shock and I just wanted to run to the ladies' room and have a good cry. It truly was an awkward moment for me, and I contemplated punching him in the nose.

I remember driving home that evening and talking to my husband about how people can say very hurtful things without realizing it. I'm sure this man, if he knew I couldn't have children and understood all the painful infertility tests I'd undergone, would never have made his comment. However, his comment still hurt.

What do we do when thoughtless comments are made? We can be mad and hold grudges; however, in the end the person we hurt the most is ourself. When it happened to me, I had to ask; *"What would the Savior do?"*

He would forgive and understand that the individual who made the remark had no idea what I had gone through. If he did, he most likely would never have made the comment. Forgive and move forward. This is not easy, but it is the best choice to make.

Colossians 3:16-17

Let the word of Christ dwell in you richly in all wisdom; teaching and admonishing one another in psalms and hymns and spiritual songs, singing with grace in your hearts to the Lord.

And whatsoever ye do in word or deed, do all in the name of the Lord Jesus, giving thanks to God and the Father by him.

■■■

When Jimmy was three years old, I signed up for a craft class called 'Making Christmas crafts with your children'. I was thoroughly loving my role as a new mother and couldn't wait to take this class so I could provide a special December month for Jimmy where he and I could make fun crafts together for Christmas.

The class was filled with so many great and creative ideas and when it was over, I couldn't wait to tell the teacher how much I enjoyed her class and appreciated all of her fantastic suggestions. After thanking her, she thanked me for attending and said, "It's a lot of work to go through for just one child. If it were me, I'm not sure I would do it."

As you can imagine, I was shocked by her comment. She was a mother of six children and was expecting her seventh, and probably didn't have a clue about how difficult it was for me to even have one child. Once again, I felt like crying, but instead, I tried to hold my head up and look for the Savior's footsteps and remember…she didn't understand my challenges and I probably didn't understand hers.

The important thing was she gave of her time and talents. Jimmy and I benefitted from my attending her class. Together we proudly displayed our crafts around our home that year and I had the satisfaction of knowing that I had provided some wonderful Christmas memories for my dear son.

Golden Rule

Do unto others as you would have them do unto you.

Chapter 6

My son, Jimmy, loved life and always had never ending energy. We discovered as he was growing up that he reacted differently to things than other children and he had a difficult time staying focused. We soon learned that he had ADD with hyperactivity.

Because of his excitability, the boys in our neighborhood made fun of him and didn't want to play with him. As a parent, it was heartbreaking to watch him try to fit in and constantly be rejected by his peers. When Jimmy got his first two-wheeled bicycle and was learning how to ride it, the neighborhood boys thought it would be funny to turn on their hose and spray water at him causing him to fall off of his bike.

This was the first of many never-ending cruel pranks the neighborhood boys pulled on him. To prevent these situations from happening, I decided to go and pick up boys from our church and bring them to our home so Jimmy would have some nice friends to play with. In spite of my doing this, the neighborhood bullies continued to throw eggs or water balloons into our backyard where Jimmy and his friends were trying to play.

Whenever there was a school holiday, I would dread it because I knew our home would become a target for the neighborhood bullies. Numerous times our front door and garage door were egged, as well as, our mailbox got filled with dog feces or other unpleasant things.

I tried talking to the parents of the bullies with no success. I was at my wit's end at this point and felt like I was losing an uphill battle. I remember going into my bedroom and kneeling in prayer where I cried and pleaded with the Lord for His help. I continued to pray for the next few days like I've never prayed before. I finally received an answer to my prayers as I was working around the house doing my daily chores. It came as an impression as follows; *"Do something they don't expect."*

Do something they don't expect...why...I just want to throw eggs at them! At least let me turn the hose on them or anything else rotten I can think of. Why can't I do that? I then felt the following impression; *"Because that's what they would expect you to do."* The more I thought about it, the more I knew the answer I had received did come from the Lord. *What wouldn't they expect? They wouldn't expect me to be nice to them that's for sure.*

As I continued to ponder this over in my mind, an idea came to me that I thought would work. I had a reputation in my church and family for making the most delicious, melt-in-your-mouth chocolate chip cookies! I decided to make a dozen cookies for each of the bullies and I would deliver them personally. I have to admit that while making them, I did consider adding some ex-lax to the batter, but I controlled myself and didn't do it!

In the middle of my baking, Jimmy and my daughter, Shelby, came into the kitchen to sample some of the finished goods. While eating and watching, they wanted to know who all the plates of cookies were for.

"I'm making a plate of cookies for each of the neighborhood bullies" I announced. If looks could kill, I would be ten feet under from the look I got from Jimmy. "I understand how you must feel about this, Jimmy." I hurried to explain how I had prayed and was surprised at the answer I received. At this point, I was willing to trust Heavenly Father and do anything I could to keep the bullies from torturing our family. "I understand if you don't like what I'm doing, but I'm asking you to support me while I try to see if Heavenly Father will help us to end all of the awful things we've been going through."

Reluctantly, Jimmy finally agreed it was worth a try…as long as he didn't have to deliver the cookies or say anything to the bullies. With the plates of cookies all packaged, I was ready to go out the door. Before leaving, I knelt once again in prayer, asking for help that all would go well.

As I walked up to the first bully's home, I saw that his father was working in the front yard. I greeted him with a smile and asked if Sam was at home. He studied me suspiciously, and asked why I wanted to see Sam. I explained that I had made a plate of cookies for him and I wanted to forgive him for all of the mean things he had done to Jimmy and our family and ask him if he would be willing to start over with a clean slate. Needless to say, that is not what he expected. He said, "Sam doesn't deserve a plate of cookies. I don't know why you made them for him. He has been very mean to your son."

I agreed and I told him I was willing to forgive Sam and wanted to start over. He shook his head in disbelief and went inside returning with his son. Sam looked very uncomfortable when he saw me. I greeted him with my best smile and said, "Hello Sam. I'm sure I'm the last person you expected to see. I made these cookies for you and I want you to know that I forgive you for all the mean things you've done to Jimmy and our family. I know deep inside you are a nice person and I'm hoping we can start over. You don't have to be friends with Jimmy, but I'm asking that you leave him alone. He has a right to be able to ride his bike down the street without being knocked off with a hose of water. He has a right to play in our yard with friends without you throwing eggs and garbage at him. I don't think you would like it if someone did those things to you. I'm sure you think I might have put something awful in these cookies to get even with you. To be honest, Sam, I did consider it. If you want, you can pick any cookie on this plate and I will eat it to prove to you that they are good cookies."

Sam actually smiled at this point and reached out to take the plate of cookies. I thanked him and turned to walk home. His father shook his head while mumbling something. I didn't mind because I knew I was doing what the Lord had instructed me to do.

I made my visits to the other bullies' homes with similar results. It was now time to wait and see what would happen after my effort of trying to *"love my enemies."*

All was quiet on the home front for the next week. I continued to drive my children to and from school and several times on the way home, as we drove through the neighborhood, we did encounter one or two of the bullies. I always waved like they were my best friends and for the first few weeks I received a third finger salute. The gesture always upset Jimmy. He let me know that I was not smart for trying to be friends with these boys. I continued to wave and be nice, and I'm thrilled to report that after a month, the third finger salute stopped and I started to receive warm greetings whenever we drove by.

To this day, the bullying stopped and our home has not been vandalized anymore with eggs and garbage. I learned a valuable lesson that when I trust and choose to follow in my Savior's footsteps, the results I receive are better than I could have ever imagined!

Golden Rule

Do unto others as you would have them do unto you.

■■

I am sad to report that my son, Jimmy, was killed by a hit-and-run driver in Santa Ana, California on July 4, 2020. Due to Covid-19, the legal system has been tied up and no current action has been taken against the driver.

This has been a heartbreaking situation to cope with in losing Jimmy like this. I feel like I've gone through every emotion that a parent can experience. In order to keep going each day, I have had to turn this situation over to the Lord and try to have faith that justice will be served in the Lord's time. I am trying to follow the Savior's footsteps in learning to love and forgive the individual who killed my son.

I'm grate for the gospel of Jesus Christ and for the knowledge I have that there is life after death to help me now through this time of separation and grief.

1 Peter 3:10-18

For he that will love life, and see good days, let him refrain his tongue from evil, and his lips that they speak no guile.

Let him eschew evil, and do good; let him seek peace, and ensue it.

For the eyes of the Lord are over the righteous, and his ears are open unto their prayers: but the face of the Lord is against them that do evil.

And who is he that will harm you, if ye be followers of that which is good?

But and if ye suffer for righteousness' sake, happy are ye: and be not afraid of their terror, neither be troubled;

But sanctify the Lord God in your hearts: and be ready always to give an answer to every man that asketh you a reason of the hope that is in you with meekness and fear.

Having a good conscience; that, whereas they speak evil of you, as of evildoers, they may be ashamed that falsely accuse your good conversation in Christ.

For it is better, if the will of God be so, that ye suffer for well doing, than for evil doing.

For Christ also hath once suffered for sins, the just for the unjust, that he might bring us to God, being put to death in the flesh, but quickened by the spirit.

Chapter 7

I was blessed to be the mother of two children, Jimmy and Shelby. When Shelby was born, her doctor told us she had a condition called a 'click hip'. He referred us to an orthopedic surgeon that advised that her hip had not formed completely while she was in the womb. By placing her hips into a brace for six months, it would allow the socket to finish developing so that her hip wouldn't slip out when she began to walk.

We were so thrilled to be blessed with a baby daughter that we happily agreed to do whatever was necessary to help her have the best life possible. After wearing a brace for six months, she then wore a body harness and brace that assisted her as she learned how to crawl and finally walk.

If we had not complied with these medical procedures, Shelby would have walked with a severe limp. We did notice that occasionally she did walk with a little hiccup in her step; however, we thought it matched her cute bubbly personality.

When Shelby was in first grade, I received a note from her teacher requesting a parent/teacher conference. I agreed to meet with her as soon as possible and couldn't help wondering what the teacher wanted to discuss with me.

After making pleasantries for a few minutes, her teacher became very serious and came right to the point. "Are you aware that your daughter has a very sexy walk for a first grader? I thought I should bring it to your attention so you can correct it right now. If you don't, you're going to have boy problems with her when she gets older."

When I realized the teacher was referring to her occasional limp, I started to feel very angry inside and wanted to verbally attack this teacher for being so petty. She had no clue about all of the medical procedures we had gone through, and to assume Shelby was deliberately trying to walk sexy to attract attention, was more than I thought I could bear. I suddenly remembered my commitment to follow the Savior's example and walk in His footsteps. I inhaled deeply in order to get control of my anger and my words.

When I exhaled, I carefully said; "Thank you so much for you concern about Shelby. I can assure you that she is not trying to walk sexy to attract attention. I'd like to tell you about her birth and the medical procedures we've gone through with her." For the next five minutes or longer, I enlightened her about why Shelby had a sexy walk. "So, you see, it is a wonderful miracle that she can walk and run and do all the things she can do. If it makes her sexy, I'm grateful! I appreciate your concern and want you to know that for right now we don't need to worry. The future may be another matter, and I will deal with that when it comes. Thank you for being her teacher and I know we're going to have a wonderful year together."

The good news is, we did have a wonderful year. Her teacher realized that Shelby was a normal girl who loved to run and play and do all the fun things that little girls do in first grade.

I went home feeling good that I hadn't lost my temper, and instead, had followed the Savior's example and walked in His footsteps explaining kindly the reason for Shelby's sexy walk!

James 1:19

Wherefore, my beloved brethren, let every man be swift to hear, slow to speak, slow to wrath.

Chapter 8

After twenty-one years of marriage, I found my life turning in a new direction due to a recent divorce. A few years later I remarried and along with my new husband, I was delighted to add two girls and a boy, making a total of five children to my newly blended family. I was excited because Ed's children were very close in age to my two children. Nic was a year younger than Jimmy, his daughter, Kim, was a year older than Shelby, and Laura was six days older than Shelby.

We soon discovered that Laura had thoroughly enjoyed being the youngest child in the family and wasn't pleased when she learned that she was six days older than Shelby, pushing her out of the position of being the youngest. Shelby, on the other hand was so thrilled to have more siblings that she would gladly trade birthdays with Laura so Laura could continue being the youngest child. To complicate matters, some relatives started to refer to Laura and Shelby as our twins due to their closeness in age, which didn't make Laura happy.

We managed to get through the first few months of our new family life without too many challenges and soon began moving into the phase where everyone became relaxed with each other and life wasn't about going to Disneyland every day. There were chores that needed to be done on a daily basis and mom and dad had work responsibilities.

As a mother, I had established a routine with my two children, and as I tried to incorporate it with my new children, I often heard comments like; *"We don't do things like that when we're at our mom's house,"* or *"I don't live here all the time so I shouldn't have to do that,"* or *"I don't want to,"* and *"I don't have to."* I had heard some unpleasant rumors about being a stepfamily, and now I was finding out firsthand why they could be so challenging. I grew up loving fairy tales and remembered vividly how the role of a stepmother was viewed. The last reputation I wanted was to be looked at as an evil, selfish stepmother and was now beginning to feel a lot more empathy for the stepmother.

One afternoon when I came home from work, I walked into the house to see what I considered a disaster area. Breakfast and lunch dishes were still scattered all over the kitchen sinks and table, food had been left out, beds weren't made, games had been played with and left out on the floor, and the TV was blaring so loud I couldn't hear myself think.

I walked over to the TV and turned it off while asking as nicely as I could, "What happened today?" No one had an answer, so I proceeded to give some work assignments and everyone got busy except Laura. I asked her to get up and begin helping and she told me in no uncertain terms; "NO" and marched off to her room. I followed her and quickly learned a valuable lesson. She was a solidly built girl and was extremely strong. When I attempted to push her door open and couldn't, I realized she was a lot stronger than I was (which of course I didn't want her to know that), so I retreated, and began worrying about what I was going to do about it.

At this point, I definitely needed a new game plan and divine intervention on how I should proceed so I went to my bedroom where I began to pray. As I prayed, I also pondered the question, "What would the Savior do? How can I follow in His footsteps?"

I reflected that the Savior never forced His way upon anyone. He shared experiences and then demonstrated the perfect example of how He would do things so His followers would know what to do. As I thought about this, I remembered how the girls were always asking for money to buy things; however, hadn't grasped the concept that you need to work and earn the money first. Ed and I, along with our two sons, were the ones working outside of the home each day while the girls were at home having a free-for-all. Suddenly a new idea was beginning to take form and I was excited to gather as a family to present it.

Our family night went well and I introduced the new concept where the girls would have the opportunity to work and earn money each day by doing their assigned chores. They also had their free agency to choose whether to do their work or not. I related it to my job…where if I went and worked, I would get paid. If I chose to stay home, then I wouldn't receive any pay because I hadn't put time and effort into working that day.

Each day when I would arrive home from work, I would immediately inspect the home and mark the work chart giving credit for the work that was completed. If someone had chosen not to do their chores, anyone else at that point could do their work and would receive credit for doing so. Every Friday would be payday and the girls that worked would receive their pay for the days they had worked.

The first week proceeded as I expected it to with Kim and Shelby doing their work faithfully each day, and when Laura didn't do her work, they eagerly volunteered to do her chores so they could earn extra money. Everyone was happy, including me, because I didn't come home to a house in chaos. I also wasn't considered the evil stepmother…that was until the first Friday came and it was payday. Kim and Shelby received their income, plus extra for completing Laura's work. Laura pouted and fussed, and I gave Ed the look that if he slipped Laura any money, he would be doing all of the housework for the next month.

The following day, Saturday, we took the girls to the mall and everyone was happy except Laura. She had to sit and watch Kim and Shelby spend their money on clothes or toys and couldn't participate in buying any special treats. I was sad to see Laura be so unhappy because of her personal choices; but this story does have a happy ending. From that day forward, Laura did her work each and every day and couldn't wait for payday so she could enjoy going shopping on Saturday!

I can't tell you how grateful I am for the Savior and all the wonderful lessons He taught. By following the Savior's example and walking in His footsteps, I was able to bring peace and joy into my home which helped all of us to live in harmony.

2 Thessalonians 3:10

For even when we were with you, this we commanded you, that if any would not work, neither should he eat.

Revelation 22:12

And behold, I come quickly; and my reward is with me, to give every man according as his work shall be.

....

While building our blended family, we experienced what I call many growing moments. We were fortunate to be able to have all of the children live with us during the summer, and during the school year, we had Ed's three children every other weekend.

Sometimes I felt like his children treated Ed and I like Santa Claus when we would pick them up. As each climbed into the car, they would verbally shout out all the things they wanted Ed and I to buy for them that weekend. After several repeat performances of this behavior, I decided we needed to have a family meeting as soon as possible.

When we arrived home, we gathered around the table and I told the children that we weren't Santa Claus and would appreciate being greeted with a nice *"Hello" or "It's good to see you,"* and not an immediate assault of everything they wanted and expected.

As we listened and talked about all of our feelings, we came up with a good plan. Each child had mentioned something special they would really like to have. We decided that a fair plan would be that they needed to earn the money for half the item and we would pay for the other half. Everyone was excited and for the next few months, the chores were completed well and in a timely manner.

The exciting part about our plan was the children had the opportunity to window shop for the items they wanted when we would be out on our Saturday excursions and they knew down to the penny how much they needed to save before they would be ready to make their purchase. Once each child had their half saved, they would show us their savings and we would arrange a time that we could take them shopping.

I noticed that when each child paid for half the item, we would let the store owner know that they had worked and saved for their purchase. It gave them great satisfaction to know they had worked for their special purchase, and I noticed over time that they appreciated and took better care of their new belonging because they had worked hard for it.

As summer was coming to an end that year, we had a family counsel and discussed what the clothing budget would be for the upcoming school year. Ed and I would buy each child a new pair of school shoes, underwear, and at least three to four new outfits. Anything else they would have to work and save for.

When it was Laura's turn to go school shopping, she seemed very unhappy about something. I remember noticing that the special item she had wanted and saved for earlier in the summer was a new pair of very expensive Skechers shoes. After buying them, she didn't wear them very often. When I asked her why she didn't wear them, she told me she didn't want them to get dirty.

When we had purchased new school shoes for Kim and Shelby, I could see that Laura was angry by her facial expressions and her body language. I soon discovered on Laura's shopping day for school clothes what had made her so upset. After purchasing her school clothes and underwear, I asked her where she wanted to go shopping for her new school shoes. She looked at me with the most puzzled expression and said, "I thought my special purchase of Skechers was my school shoes."

I wrapped my arms around her and hugged her when I suddenly understood why she had been so angry. "Laura, that was your special purchase that you worked for…not your school shoes. You can wear them any time you want and your dad and I are still going to buy you a brand-new pair of shoes for school. Is that why you haven't been wearing them?"

She nodded her head and had tears of joy in her eyes. My heart went out to this dear, sweet girl who thought that her special purchase had to also count for her school shoes. It taught me another valuable lesson. Even though your children are looking at you and listening to you, their understanding of what you have said may not be the same as what you thought you had communicated.

In this chapter I learned a lot from my new children. I accused them of treating me like Santa Claus. It got me to thinking about how many times I ask for too many things when I'm praying. I wondered if Heavenly Father might feel like I'm treating Him like Santa Claus. I have prayed for forgiveness for asking for too much, and I'm now trying to do a better job of focusing on the things I say when I'm praying so He will know I'm trying to talk to Him the way I want my children to talk to me. It's fascinating all the things we learn when we follow in our Savior's footsteps.

Romans 8:28

And we know that all things work together for good to them that love God, to them who are the called according to his purpose.

Chapter 9

Ed and I were married for a little over fifteen years when I received word at work that he had passed away from an enlarged heart. It came as a huge shock and was a difficult challenge to adjust to right away. All of our children were grown and on their own and I decided it would be best if I continued working. I did so, not only to support myself, but I needed to keep busy in order to handle my sorrow and loneliness.

Three years had gone by since his passing and I was still struggling with loneliness. My daughter, Shelby, encouraged me to look for a new companion, but I wasn't sure if I was ready for another marriage. I finally decided to try some online dating through a church website and was fortunate to meet Dean. His wife had recently passed away from a long illness and he was suffering from loneliness as well. Our personalities and goals matched so we decided to get married.

After returning from our honeymoon, we decided that we would live in his home and would sell mine. Dean had a Siamese cat named Amelia that he absolutely loved and adored and had spoiled rotten. She was not happy to see me and reacted jealously of my presence in the home. When we were getting ready for bed the first night back from our honeymoon, Amelia decided to let me know exactly how she felt about me. Dean and I were standing side by side talking and she leaped off the bed flying between us, and narrowly missing my head and shoulders.

Needless to say, it shocked me and I wasn't very happy about it. I could see a look of worry in Dean's eyes, and at that point, I figured I would be the one he would put out the door first so, I better come up with a plan on how I was going to get along with Amelia.

The interesting part of this story is animals have always loved me. I don't know what it is about me that they find so fascinating, but animals seem to always be drawn to me and tend to follow me around. I had even kidded Dean before we got married that Amelia would probably end up liking me more than him. I was certainly having my doubts about that now.

Before going to sleep that night, I closed my eyes and pondered; *what would the Savior do in this situation? The first impression that came to me was LOVE. Yes, I was positive that the Savior would show more love to Amelia, and that is what I must do as well in order to reassure her that she would always have an important place in our home. Amelia needed to see unconditional love from me in order to convince her that I wasn't a threat to her happiness and security. Was this going to be easy? Absolutely not, especially if she continued to try to take my head off. I had faith in my Savior and the impression that I was given, and was willing to try to see this through.*

Over the next few months, Amelia tested me over and over to see how I would react to her antics. I have to admit that there were many times that I thought about giving up. No matter how sweet or how kind I tried to be, she continued to be friendly up to a point, and then she would nip at me or jump off my lap leaving scratch marks.

I thought about my relationship with previous animals I had had and remembered that consistency is a key factor to helping your pet become the kind of pet you want them to be. I worked at being kind and loving, and when she did things I didn't like, I ignored her and only gave her attention for the loving things she did.

This seemed to be the magic that finally began to turn my relationship with her around. She missed the kind things I would do for her when she acted naughty and she slowly began to realize that if she wanted my attention and affection, she needed to act like a loving kitty. It's been fun to watch the transformation in her, and especially rewarding when family members have dropped by for a visit and have noticed the changes in her better behavior as well. She is one of the most beautiful cats you'll ever see and now is as beautiful on the inside as the outside.

In our third year of marriage, Dean and I started noticing that Amelia started choosing me over him. We laugh and tease about it now, and I realize it has only come after many years of treating her like I knew the Savior would by always showing love and kindness. It was a very slow process, but well worth the effort now that there is mutual love and trust between Amelia and I.

I have learned once again that by following in the Savior's footsteps, we can also have loving and rewarding relationships with our animals.

Golden Rule

Do unto others as you would have them do unto you.

Matthew 7:12

Therefore all things whatsoever ye would that men should do to you, do ye even so to them: for this is the law and the prophets.

Chapter 10

I have always enjoyed writing and was thrilled when I received my first diary as a child. Mrs. Dayton, my first-grade teacher, thought I had quite an imagination. When she signed my autograph book, she encouraged me to pursue my writing talent. I thought I would definitely do that when I got around to it...which wasn't until 2011 at the age of sixty! It is now 2023 and I have a total of twelve books that have been published.

A few years ago, I decided to try my hand at doing my own advertising to help promote my books on Facebook. I created an ad for my most recent published book on Facebook and was very pleased with my verbiage and decided to conclude it by adding a picture of the cover of my book. I tried to preview my finished ad, but couldn't figure that part out. I went ahead and submitted my ad and was very embarrassed when I saw the finished ad as it appeared on Facebook.

The picture of my book cover was completely blurred and looked like something a two-year old would have submitted. I was hoping everyone who viewed it would just notice what I said and would overlook my lack of expertise in graphic arts. No such luck!

Fortunately, it was only a two-week ad; however, I had more attention in those two weeks than I wanted. I hate to admit that the teenagers who are so proficient at anything to do with computers and posting social media had a field day with my ad...or should I say...my lack of talent in posting a clear picture.

My first reaction was to fire back some verbal nasties; but then I remembered that I'm trying to follow in the Savior's footsteps. As I wondered what I should do, I prayed and once again asked; *what would the Savior do? The immediate impression was; show love, be kind, laugh at your mistakes.*

As I read through the many derogatory comments on my ad's picture, I was once again humiliated at my attempt to try to post an inviting ad and prayed for help to be nice with my reply.

A young man named, Mark, posted a particularly nasty comment so, I stopped and responded as follows; "I'm sorry the picture came out so fuzzy. When I wrote the ad, I asked if I could see it and I wasn't allowed to. When I did see it, I felt bad that it came out the way it did. Hopefully you read the things I said and can overlook my graphic art abilities. I appreciate your visit to my website. Hope you have a fantastic day."

Mark responded as follows; "Oh I didn't mean to act that way. I feel sorry. It's ok."

My response; "You are a kind person and I can tell that! If we saw each other, we could both have a good laugh over it. No worries, Mark, and thanks."

My eyes immediately filled with tears of gratitude for not acting on my first impression and firing back with nasty remarks of my own; but instead, remembering my goal of trying to follow in the Savior's footsteps. What a difference it has made in my life. I behave so much better and those around me respond positively to my wanting to be like the Savior.

There were a lot more negative remarks made about my posting...*such a terrible picture,* and I responded kindly to the responses. I learned almost immediately that when I responded with love, kindness, and understanding, admitting my mistakes, people stopped attacking me and usually responded back with a kind remark, or they chose to just let it go. It has been a rewarding experience.

Luke 6:38

Give, and it shall be given unto you; good measure, pressed down and shaken together, and running over, shall men give into your bosom.

For with the same measure that ye mete withal it shall be measured to you again.

PART 2

Putting the Lord First in Your Life

Chapter 11

Before getting married, I was called to teach a young women's class of twelve- and thirteen-year-olds. I had moved to California, gotten my own apartment and job, and was learning quickly about the challenges of having to live on a budget and making every penny I earned count.

After giving a Sunday lesson to my young women on always paying their tithing first, I was faced with a new dilemma of my own when I arrived home from work a few days later. I was going through my mail and nearly fainted when I received a bill from the gas company advising me that they had forgotten to charge me for a new service hookup fee. One of the first things that went through my mind was; *how am I going to pay for this extra bill?* My budget was stretched to its limit and I wasn't sure what I was going to do. I had always been taught to be honest in my dealings and to put the Lord first.

My thoughts went back to the lesson I had given to my young women's class and I thought; *I can't tell them to do something I'm not willing to do myself.* For the next couple of days, I worried constantly about how I was going to stretch my next paycheck to cover everything. As I continued to worry, I remembered what my mother always taught me while growing up. *The Lord will never get in debt to you; you will always be in debt to Him.*

With that thought in mind, I knew what I was going to do. When I received my next paycheck, I paid my tithing first along with my other bills, and I decided to wait on paying the gas hookup fee, hoping I could tighten my budget enough to pay it on my next paycheck. I dreaded driving to the post office to mail my bills because I worried about whether the gas company might shut my service off. Instead, I tried to focus my thinking on trusting the Lord and having faith. It brought to mind another principle I had been taught and it goes something like this; *after the trial of your faith, then come the blessings.*

On my drive home from the post office, I prayed that the Lord wouldn't forget me and asked for help to find a way to meet my other obligation. The following day was Saturday and I was busy cleaning my apartment, going grocery shopping, and getting ready for Sunday. When I checked my mail late in the day, I saw a letter from my car insurance company. I started to panic as I opened it, worried that it might be another forgotten bill. To my surprise, it was a refund check for a dollar more than the gas hookup fee due to an overpayment on my policy. When I moved from Utah to California,

I had made an extra payment to the Utah office and they notified the California office that I had prepaid before I moved. I wanted to make sure the policy was in effect during my move and had forgotten that there might be a refund coming my way.

I jumped for joy and uttered a quick prayer of thanks to the Lord for coming to my rescue. The timing was perfect and I couldn't be more thankful. I looked forward to going to church the next day so I could share my tithing experience with the young women.

I know that when you put the Lord first in your life, He will always open the way for good things to happen.

Malachi 3:10

Bring ye all the tithes into the storehouse, that there may be meat in mine house, and prove me now herewith, saith the Lord of hosts, if I will not open you the windows of heaven, and pour you out a blessing, that there shall not be room enough to receive it.

Ether 12:6

And now, I, Moroni, would speak somewhat concerning these things, faith is things

which are hoped for and not seen; wherefore, dispute not because ye see not, for ye receive no witness until after the trial of your faith.

Chapter 12

Becoming a mother to my dear son, Jimmy, was an exciting time in my life! I had no idea how quickly babies could dirty their clothes at one end or the other. One of my biggest challenges was having enough money to keep up with the purchase of formula, diapers, and laundry soap to manage all the wash that was now required.

It was a Monday morning and I was walking up and down the aisles of the grocery store while carefully calculating my purchases so I didn't go over our family budget. Along with formula, diapers, and laundry soap, I still had a couple of meals I needed to work into the weekly budget, as well as, a few last-minute items to pick up.

As I was rounding the corner of the baby aisle, I met a lady from our church who told me about a sister in our neighborhood who was going through a challenging time and needed some help. She asked if I could take a meal in to her family that night and I readily agreed. Her family was larger than mine, and by the time I placed all of the items in my cart that I would need to make dinner for them, I knew that I didn't have enough money for everything.

I returned some of the formula to the baby aisle and I decided not to purchase the laundry soap. I still had a little laundry soap at home; however, I knew it wouldn't be enough to make it through the whole week. I was concerned about my decision to help and said a quick prayer that the Lord would provide a way for it to all work out.

I remembered once again the wonderful advice of my mother when she said, *the Lord will never get in debt to me; I will always be in debt to Him.* With that in mind, I continued on my way making a meal for the sister who needed help.

When I went outside to pick up the mail that afternoon, I couldn't believe my eyes when I opened the mailbox and there were two boxes of sample laundry soap waiting for me! I could barely contain my excitement and as I lifted my eyes heavenward, thanking Heavenly Father for once again answering my prayers. Tears of joy began to flow down my cheeks as I thought about skipping back to my front door.

I know that we have a Father in Heaven who is aware of our needs and won't hesitate to pour down the blessings of heaven when we need them. By putting the Lord first in my life, I once again, experienced His miracles firsthand!

Ether 12:16-18

Yea, and even all they who wrought miracles wrought them by faith, even those who were before Christ and also those who were after.

And it was by faith that the three disciples obtained a promise that they should not taste of death; and they obtained not the promise until after their faith.

And neither at any time hath any wrought miracles until after their faith; wherefore they first believed in the son of God.

Chapter 13

My grandfather Horman loved music and hoped that his grandchildren would inherit his love of music. When I was living in California, I had the opportunity of taking piano lessons from a world-renowned pianist, Joseph Ogle. Before he would accept me as a student, I had to audition for him and make a commitment to practice at least two to three hours a day. I was delighted when he called to let me know that I had been accepted as a student. I could only afford to take lessons for a few months, but thought it would be well worth the experience.

A short time after I began my piano lessons, I was asked by my church to be in charge of a special program for all the young women, ages 12 to 18. This program was important because it welcomed the new twelve-year-old girls coming into the program and it only occurred once a year. There was a lot of preparation that required my attention to ensure that the program would be ready. I soon realized I didn't have enough time to do both my piano practicing and prepare for this program.

I chose to prepare for the young women's program and have faith that the Lord would bless me when it was time to go to my next piano lesson. When the day of my piano lesson arrived, I hadn't practiced at all. I prayed that I would get a phone call cancelling my lesson; however, the phone never rang. I also prayed for a miracle that when I sat down in front of Mr. Ogle's piano my fingers would miraculously play the songs perfectly.

While driving to Mr. Ogle's studio, I continued to worry and could even picture him terminating me on the spot. I parked my car and began the long walk to his door, praying with each step I took.

Suddenly, I heard the front door of his studio open and I saw Mr. Ogle running outside in a panic. I was surprised to see him looking so agitated, and was curious about why he was so upset. When he saw me, he hurried over to me and said; "Christy, I am so sorry that you drove all the way over here. I tried to reach you by phone, but you must have already left your home when I tried to call. The studio was so cold this morning, and when I turned on the furnace, it made a terrible noise and smoke began pouring out of the vents. It's too smoky in there to have your piano lesson today. I apologize and hope you will forgive me for this inconvenience."

As you can imagine, I wanted to jump for JOY! I let Mr. Ogle know it was okay and I would happily see him the following week. I tried very hard not to skip back to my car from relief. As soon as I climbed into my car, I laughed, I cried, and I immediately began to say a prayer of thanks! As I said my prayer, I told Heavenly Father that He definitely has a thing for furnaces, and couldn't help laughing when I remembered the story of Shadrach, Meshach, and Abednego when they were cast into the midst of a burning fiery furnace. Regardless of what method He chose to help me, I will be forever grateful that He delivered me from my piano lesson that day!

I know from my own personal experiences that when we put the Lord first in our lives, He will bless us and reward our efforts. I have experienced this so many times in my own life and know it's true.

Daniel 3:15-18

Now if ye be ready that at what time ye hear the sound of the cornet, flute, harp, sackbut, psaltery, and dulcimer, and all kinds of musick, ye fall down and worship the image which I had made; well: but if ye worship not, ye shall be cast the same hour into the midst of a burning fiery furnace; and who is that God that shall deliver you out of my hands?

Shadrach, Meshach, and Abednego, answered and said to the king, O

Nebuchadnezzar, we are not careful to answer thee in this matter.

If it be so, our God whom we serve is able to deliver us from the burning fiery furnace, and golden image which thou has set up.

Joshua 24:15

And if it seem evil unto you to serve the Lord, choose you this day whom ye will serve; whether the gods which your fathers served that were on the other side of the flood, or the gods of the Amorites, in whose land ye dwell: but as for me and my house, we will serve the Lord.

PART 3

The Joy of Service

Chapter 14

My grandmother Horman passed away when I was eight years old and it was difficult to see my grandfather Horman grieve her loss. He later married a wonderful lady named, June. She was so loving and accepting of all of her new grandchildren. My sister, Lawanna, and I had been cleaning my grandfather's home each week and felt fortunate that grandma June wanted us to continue. She always made our cleaning visits extra special by leaving out treats or loving notes for us.

When Christmas time came that year, Lawanna and I wanted to do something extra special for them. We had purchased treats and small presents and Lawanna had sewn some homemade Christmas stockings. We knew they would be coming to our home on Christmas Eve for dinner and we planned to excuse ourselves after dinner to run some last-minute Christmas errands.

With all of the Christmas excitement, we were able to excuse ourselves and Lawanna drove us to their home where we proceeded to let ourselves in with our cleaning key. We scurried around the house like Christmas elves laughing and decorating and leaving Christmas cheer everywhere we went.

This was my first time of really giving selfless service at Christmas time and it was fun and exciting. Lawanna and I giggled with true joy and I had never felt the Christmas spirit so strong. When we got back home and settled down with our family to read the Savior's birth out of Luke in the New Testament, I felt like I knew the real reason for celebrating the Christmas season. I could feel the Savior's love for me and each person sitting in the room. Tears of joy and gratitude fell from my eyes that special Christmas Eve. I felt the true joy of service and couldn't wait to do it again!

Mosiah 2:17

And behold, I tell you these things that ye may learn wisdom; that ye may learn that when ye are in the service of your fellow beings ye are only in the service of your God.

Chapter 15

When our son, Jimmy, was small my husband and I got to know a young man in our church who felt frustrated because he wasn't able to participate in a lot of activities because his bicycle was old and it would cost too much to repair it. He later confided in me that he would like to attend the young men activities but wouldn't because his bike was old and outdated, and he was too embarrassed to ride it.

Christmas was around the corner and I couldn't help thinking about his situation. One evening after my husband and I had put Jimmy to bed, I brought up the subject of Jeff and told my husband how much Jeff wanted a bicycle. I said I wouldn't mind taking any Christmas money we had set aside for ourselves and use it to purchase a new bike for him. I was thrilled when my husband thought it was a great idea and he would stop by the next day to check out bicycles on his way home from work.

The following day I felt such joy and excitement and couldn't wait for my husband to get home. He was as happy as I was and when the bicycle shop learned that we were buying it for a boy that needed help, they agreed to sell it for their cost and would also deliver it to his home on

Christmas Eve so the gift could remain anonymous. With the money we saved on the bike, we purchased a beautiful Christmas floral arrangement and had it sent to the home along with some Christmas goodies!

Once again, I was able to feel the true Christmas spirit of loving and giving! It stands out as one of my favorite Christmas memories.

Luke 9:24

For whosoever will save his life shall lose it: but whosoever will lose his life for my sake, the same shall save it.

Chapter 16

It is always easier to share experiences where I have given service to others. I would now like to share an experience where I was the recipient of service and how it made me feel.

I had lost my job in July of 2001 due to the company having financial struggles. I had just turned fifty and was finding that potential employers liked my work experience; however, they expressed concern that I wouldn't stay with their company if something better came along. I heard that similar statement for four months and didn't obtain a job until November of that year. It was a job as a receptionist where I was making less than half of what I had been previously making. I was grateful to have a job and figured I would re-budget my bills and get a second job to help supplement my income.

I lost a lot of weight during this time because I could only afford to eat one good meal a day. I snacked on nuts and fruits to keep me going whenever I would get too hungry. Christmas was fast approaching and I tried not to let on to friends or family how bleak things really were for me. I managed to pay my bills and was barely staying afloat. My children were grownup at this time and I lived on my own...so no one knew about my true circumstances. I remember hearing commercials on TV where they would state that people were hungry, even possibly their neighbors...and I was one of them!

My parents and my siblings had no idea what I was going through and I didn't want them to know. Christmas Eve arrived and I was grateful when my manager at work advised we would be closing the office early for Christmas. Everyone was happy and anxious to get home to family and their Christmas celebrations. I smiled and acted like I was happy too. On my way home, I stopped by Taco Bell and treated myself to a taco and ate it slowly while trying to savor and enjoy my Christmas Eve dinner.

When I got home, I gathered the plates of Christmas sugar cookies I had made and got ready to deliver them to several people who had been nice to me. I wished everyone a Merry Christmas and made my way to my final stop, the Yorks.

Mr. York invited me into their home and I couldn't help noticing the wonderful aroma of a ham baking in the oven, baked potatoes, and other Christmas delights that smelled out of this world. It brought back memories of my own Christmases when things were better for me.

I glanced wistfully at their Christmas table decorated beautifully with the finest linen and fine

China resting at each place setting. My thoughts were interrupted by Mrs. York who was carrying a medium sized wicker basket. She stopped and wished me a Merry Christmas and then extended her arms, urging me to accept the basket.

When I looked inside the basket, I gasped with surprise when I saw a ham, potatoes, and other delightful Christmas goodies nestled with care. I couldn't believe my eyes and I started to cry and could barely get my words of thanks out.

I'm pretty sure I shocked them because they obviously had no idea how hungry I was. They invited me to stay, but I humbly declined and was anxious to be on my way...however...very, very grateful.

As I walked to my car carrying my basket full of Christmas blessings, I looked up with tears of pure joy and thanked Heavenly Father for blessing me with the delicious basket of food and I offered a prayer of thanks for the service that had been given to me.

It is more blessed to give; but it is also blessed to receive when it is truly needed. I have never forgotten this gift of love and service to me.

Acts 20:35

I have shewed you all things, how that so laboring ye ought to support the weak, and to remember the words of the Lord, Jesus, how he said, It is more blessed to give than to receive.

Made in United States
Orlando, FL
03 December 2024

54932225R00048